Enjoy these beautiful scenes!

A Sinno
Rabi Sinno
Omar Sinno

the *Mississippi River*
Border to Border

Panoramas & Impressions
By: Abdul Karim Sinno, Ph.D., and Rafic Sinno, MBA, with contributions from Omar Sinno, BS

Copyright © 2010. Woodward Communications, Inc.

TELEGRAPH HERALD
Dubuque, Iowa

Publisher: James F. Normandin
Executive Editor: Brian Cooper
Project Manager: Diane Mohr
Cover/Interior Design: Rachel Rosenthal
Cover Photo: Rafic Sinno

Photos © Dr. Abdul Karim Sinno, pages 6, 7, 10-11, 12-13, 14-15, 16-17, 18-19, 20-21, 22-23, 24-25, 26, 27, 30-31, 32, 34-35, 36-37, 38, 39, 40-41, 42-43, 44-45, 46, 47, 50-51, 52-53, 54, 55, 58-59, 60-61, 62-63, 64-65, 68, 69, 74-75, 76-77, 82-83, 84-85, 86-87, 88-89, 92, 93, 94-95, 98, 99, 100-101, 102, 103, 106-109, 112, 113, 114-115, 116-117, 118-119
Photos © Rafic Sinno, pages 8-9, 28, 29, 33, 48, 49, 56-57, 64-65, 66-67, 78-79, 80-81, 96-97, 104-105
Photos © Omar Sinno, pages 70-71, 72-73, 90, 91, 110-111

www.THonline.com | www.SinnoCom.com | www.MississippiRiverBordertoBorder.com | www.MississippiRiverPanoramas.com

Title Page - Map of the Mississippi River from its source to the mouth of the Missouri. Laid down from the notes of Lieutt. Z. M. Pike by Anthony Nau. Reduced and corrected by the astronomical observations of Mr. Thompson at its source; and of Captn. M. Lewis, where it receives the waters of the Missouri. By Nichs. King. Engraved by Francis Shallus, Philadelphia, 1811. Courtesy of the Library of Congress Geography and Map Division Washington, D.C. 20540-4650 USA

ISBN 978-0-9819806-1-4

Printed in China

Dedication

To my cherished wife, Melissa.
To my beloved sons, Rafic, Omar, and Olli.
To my late beloved and ever-missed parents.

Preface

Dear Reader,

When I was in grade school, in Lebanon, over 50 years ago, my English teacher was telling us about the Mississippi River. The teacher offered a star to the first kid who could spell Mississippi correctly. I took that star and it went to my book and to my heart. This star evolved into a galaxy of panoramic views of the Mighty River spreading its beauty from North to South.

This nation has the most spectacular scenes in the world. People do not have to travel far to enjoy the beautiful attractions that the Mighty River reveals and hides. Many times, these scenes are so close to us that we take them for granted. One lady, looking at one of our panoramas, said "I have lived all my life in this city but never seen it that beautiful!" I replied: "You are looking at it every day from the same perspective. Change your outlook and everything around you will change." As I mentioned in my first book, *Treasures of the Mississippi: Panoramas and Poetic Reflections*, there is nothing that connects people like beauty and art. It is our family's mission and hope that this book brings to people beauty, happiness, and peace.

Our first book carried this mission all over the world. The book went to China, Canada, the Middle East, Japan, Korea, Germany, Iceland, Hungary, Paris, Beirut, and many other locations. The present book is wider in scope as it covers the 10 river states from Lake Itasca to the Gulf of Mexico with a focus on Iowa, Illinois and Wisconsin due to their natural geographic location around the center of the Mississippi River and due to the fact that Dubuque is the hometown we cherish.

Across the years, the Sinno family took several trips north and south. Many of the pictures you see in this book were unplanned! We simply discovered these locations by coincidence or with the unsolicited help of the local people who went out of their way to escort us to their favorite sites overlooking the river. The people who live around the river are as giving, generous, and pleasant as the river itself. We have so many stories to share about the river and its people meriting another book.

Consequently, through this book and our presentations, we are raising awareness about the Mighty River, its heritage, history, beauty, and touristic values to a variety of government agencies, educational institutions, conferences, businesses, and for non-profit organizations. We encourage everyone to invest in this national treasure. It is worth it and will pay back not only financially, but, as well, in patriotism, pride, and love to this great nation.

This book features the river in its many phases from the variant blue to the muddy brown or the reddish glow around sunsets and sunrises; you will see it as if you were with us on our journeys. All pictures are taken from land except for the panorama of Galena that shows Galena, the Mississippi and Iowa's bluffs, Pilottown, LA; and a picture of the lighthouse on the Southwest Pass as the Mississippi merges into the Gulf of Mexico. The first picture was taken from a hot-air balloon. The second and third were taken from a boat we chartered. Included are pictures of locations in different seasons. It is amazing to see the lush green of summer turning into the mystic brown of fall, and the snow white of winter (mostly in the northern states).

We invite you to visit these locations and enjoy what we experienced of beauties that neither pictures nor words can fully reveal.

Abdul Karim Sinno, Ph.D.

Thank You

Of course, our first thanks goes to God who gave us the vision, the word and the knowledge to do this work and spread the beauty of his creation. A big thank you goes to my great family: my late parents, my brothers and sisters and especially to my sister Houda Sinno.

Thanks to this great nation that gave all of us the freedom, the opportunity, and the support to produce this work—thank you America our precious home.

Thanks to my valued friend and colleague Brian Cooper of the Telegraph Herald for bringing this work to fruition; words fall short of thanking Brian. Likewise, our thanks go to Steve Fisher who, with Brian, selected this book for publication. A special thank you goes to the Telegraph Herald's managers, staff, and personnel for their support and help including Diane Mohr, Amy Gilligan, Dave Kettering, Rachel Rosenthal, and Jeremy Portje.

A special thank you goes to Anace and Polly Aossey for their continuous support, friendship, and encouragement. Thanks to our friends and colleagues Dirk Voetberg, William Conzett, Dr. Michael and Claire Lattner, Gary and Linda Olsen for their continued support and encouragement. Further thanks to Richard and Sandy Rolwes, John and Ruth Denlinger, Amy Schadle of the Fenelon Place Elevator, Sr. Mira Mosle of the Dubuque-based Sisters of Charity BVMs, and Robert and Christine Apel for their support in documenting this river.

As well, our thanks to all our friends, colleagues, business partners and affiliates and to the many others who supported us through e-mail, post cards, letters and telephone calls from all over the nation and from overseas. The list of thanks can never end due to the enormous support and encouragement from friends all over the world.

Thanks to the caring and encouraging Clarke college community. Thanks to our colleagues and students who were instrumental in encouraging and inspiring us.

Abdul Karim Sinno, Ph.D.   Rafic Sinno, MBA

$\mathcal{L}$ake Itasca, Minnesota: The majesty of the river, the trees, and the spectacular skies make me wish that I could stretch every second into eternity. After a long drive, we arrive at Lake Itasca, the mother of the Mississippi, and enter a race against daylight and weather. On this stormy evening, it is shortly before sunset. The sky is grey and then, in a minute, becomes a fascinating blue, reviving the colors of the turning trees. Lake Itasca Park is huge, windy, and mystic! The lake is petite, yet gorgeous. The rocks around her form a necklace of protecting jewels. The trees on its northern shores clone themselves into its waters, effecting a perpetual hug of the lake. As we record the beauty of the headwaters, the clouds clear for a moment. It is amazing how this little lake can bring forth this source of national pride, the Mississippi River.

emidji, Minnesota: The Mississippi does not want the easy way down. The magnificent river decides to travel upwards all the way to Bemidji. Now there are two big things in Bemidji: The Mississippi and Paul Bunyan. Where is the Mississippi? The Paul Bunyan Museum's lady tells us it is all around us: Wherever you look, it is there.

But this is a lake! Yes, this lake is Mississippi-fed; the stream gave birth to its mother lake, which graces all of Bemidji. The museum displays the mythical lumberjack's relics, including his shotgun, axe, trophy fish, and fishing rod. Go to Bemidji and experience the mix of myth and reality: Paul Bunyan and the Mississippi.

_G_rand Rapids, Minnesota: Melissa says, "You really can write a book on every inch of this land." Gaze upon the river, the turning leaves, and the serenity of this place. We take our gear and spread out, each of us capturing photos as if there was no tomorrow. Melissa invites me to her vantage point; it made me forget mine. Rafic invites both of us to his vantage point; it makes us gasp. Every image we capture is beautiful, but this one represents well the breathtaking experience.

rainerd, Minnesota: This panorama is not easy to capture. It is a difficult choice, as other scenes of the Mississippi at Brainerd are equally fascinating and compelling. I often stop shooting, just to take in the changing colors and shades before the moment escapes. On a hilltop, Rafic and I do not hear each other, but each of us is trying to point out one scene after another. Melissa, waiting for us below, enjoys other views — ones that escape us. Back in our hotel room, reviewing our images on the computer screen, we gasp repeatedly upon seeing the beauty at Brainerd.

$\mathcal{S}$auk Rapids, Minnesota: As we approach Sauk Rapids, we encounter this fantastic scene. The rocks in the river tell us that the Mississippi is still mostly shallow here. These rocks appear to be part of the beautiful hill shown. The river needs more room to grow on its trip south, so the hill volunteered its lower stretch to unite with the Mighty River.

St. Cloud, Minnesota: As we unwrap our sandwiches, we discover that we are right on the Mississippi River —what a double treat. The flowers, the beautiful skies, the turning trees and the Sinnos all are in the unity of time and place. Wherever I look, I see the beauties I cherish. I see downriver symmetry among the trees, the sky and the simple beauty that spreads across St. Cloud. Go there and discover the beauties that are particular to you. I bet that you will be happy with what you will see inside yourself as the river becomes part of your soul.

inneapolis, Minnesota: Look at all the buildings overlooking the river! They stand high on the hills, and their dwellers have an eternal view of the Mississippi. Wide and high, these buildings contain people, businesses, governments, agencies, shopping centers and the like, with a singular message: "We have a river view." This is an asset. The greater the view of the river, the greater its asking price. Why? I believe that seeing the water is soothing, relieving, and therapeutic. This is especially true when the pressure of daily exigencies overweighs little escapes that busy people may enjoy. Hence, amidst this busy life, a glimpse of the beautiful waters is a cooling diversion.

Minneapolis, Minnesota

St. Paul, Minnesota: St. Paul's Art Center is a must-visit place. No words can do this national treasure fairness. Go and discover it for yourself. Fascinated and numb over what I see in this "mini city" of art and culture, I go to one of its riverview balconies. My gaze touches upon the river, the marina, the boats, the bridges, the walkways and the roads. No matter where I look, I see art, harmony, and beauty that match the river as it flows within the big city.

$\mathcal{R}$ ed Wing, Minnesota: This community is crowded with culture, heritage and beauty! Melissa, Rafic, and I decide to take a panorama from the blufftop park. What we see is a showcase of perfection! The city spills from the bluffs to the river, whose banks contour in an S shape. The trees of Red Wing projected the pinnacle of colors and shapes — spherical, conical... and shapes that geometry has yet to discover. Quite simply, Red Wing unites beauty, art, and the Mississippi.

Lake City, Minnesota: I can't believe what I am seeing right from the highway as we enter Lake City: the clouds, the sail boats, the water, and the natural rocks' dike that extends into the waters.

They create a painting that I did not paint! I waste no time. My travels on the river taught me that a sunny day with a beautiful blue canopy can turn into a storm within minutes. The gripping formation of

clouds, the sky, the season and the time of the day make this picture a one-of-a-kind. It may never be repeated.

$\mathcal{P}$epin, Wisconsin: Opposite Lake City and slightly downriver is the Wisconsin community of Pepin, home to a lake on and of the Mississippi. We arrive a little before sunset to take in the sight of the Mississippi, the tourists, the locals, and the boats returning to the marina. The smell of fish fry from the restaurants nearby magnifies a faint appetite into a nagging hunger. The sight of parents and their children hopping on and off the boats is pleasant and moving. It is part of the happy, peaceful and pleasant American reality.

$\mathcal{A}$lma, Wisconsin: I tell Dad, "I want to stay here!" We reach the end of a cliff, and gaze upon Alma, Wabasha and Lock and Dam 4. The Mississippi hosts all these gorgeous places around it drawing circles of unmatched aesthetics. Reaching Buena Vista State Park is an exciting adventure. We ascend the steep winding road, taking in farms, cows, deer, silos, and, of course, golden fields of corn. We reflect upon the hardy nature of the farmers who converted the most savage beauty into fertile land and planted these steep hills. As we reach the overlook, I feel as if I am an alien visiting a wonderful planet for the first time.

$\mathcal{D}$akota, Minnesota: No, it is not a state. Yes, it is one of the smallest American towns on the bank of the Mississippi in Minnesota. What you see is the simplest versions of beauty and yet the most attractive. The blue river, the white clouds, and the green grass act in concert — in shape, color, and dimension — to paint a masterpiece. It is true that beauty is like love — only known when lived.

inona, Minnesota: Often, the Mississippi cedes to certain communities a generous portion of itself to form lakes and ponds that are eternally alive and beautiful. From the overlook in a blufftop park I see how the Mississippi gave way, changed course, and formed a lake. It is a place I often visit for contemplation and relaxation. I can see the city without traffic jams, streets without massive crowds, cars without choking overdoses of pollution. I can see the town the way I want it to be. Winona is one of the many places on the Mississippi that serves up a satisfying slice of beauty in this great nation.

*T*rempealeau, Wisconsin: This little town on U.S. Highway 61 is steeped in peace and tranquility. Yes, Trempealeau is small and, yes, it is pretty. As I set up my camera, I see four layers of beauty. Starting at the background, there is the guardian hill protecting its treasure. As you can see, this hill survived the Glacier. The second layer is a town that defines beauty, innocence, and simplicity. The third is the little island that forms an amazing symmetrical fractal of the guardian hill. The fourth is the curtain of trees, brushes, and shafts that bend in salute to the eternal beauty behind them.

$\mathcal{L}$ake Onalaska, Minnesota: Everything went wrong today. I escape to Lake Onalaska in search of relaxation. I know that nothing calms me down better than the sight of water. I arrive at the Mississippi-fed lake and sit on the sand, doodling meaningless shapes and lines. Gazing at the sky, I am taken by the view. The sky seems too close to the lake! The sky and the lake appear as identical shells, with an exquisite pearl in between. At the horizon they seal and close a chapter on the day. That is all I want — to think freely without restriction, to enjoy beauty without rules and to share with Mother Nature what I cannot share with humans. She is more tolerant and permissive. Quite often, I recall this scene when I am stressed. And it helps.

$\mathcal{L}$ake Onalaska, Minnesota: You need not dream when you are living one. Lake Onalaska is a dream for every passion. I often sit with a book or two on that picnic table. Those books are never opened. There is better reading at hand — that which God has written upon that peaceful piece of Heavens. I see the fisherman's dream of a big catch, the sailboat leaving a trail of triangular waves as it heads to the horizon, the branches stretching over the water and acting as small umbrellas, providing shade, shape, and substance to the scene. Lake Onalaska is like a resting place for the Mississippi River: taking a break on its journey south.

La Crosse, Wisconsin

La Crosse, Wisconsin: Yes, every tree has a present for the Mississippi River — a gift of light, blessings, and jubilee. The river at La Crosse awaits Christmas and New Year to enjoy a shore-long of celebrations. Despite the 15-below temperature, the glimmering lights across the shore bring warmth, beauty, and happiness to the heart. This scene is nothing like we have seen before — thanks to the city and the Welcome Center of La Crosse, which give a precious holiday present to all and, in particular, to the Mighty River.

43

*L*ansing, Iowa: This is not an aerial photograph. It is taken from the park at Mount Hosmer, overlooking Lansing. We frequently visit here and enjoy the breathtaking scene, relax, and pictorially document its beauty. This is the southern section of Lansing, shown a little before sunset. It takes me a long time to take this picture — a very long time! I was so fascinated with the beauty — the contours of the river; the colorful, cozy houses on its banks; the spacious green islands that spring forth from the fascinating blue water — I often had to remind myself to press the shutter button on my camera.

$\mathcal{M}$cGregor, Iowa: Pikes Peak State Park overlook is one of the most popular vantage points on the Mississippi River. The park, which sits above McGregor, is open year-round. This panorama takes in towns from two states: Marquette on the Iowa side and Prairie du Chien in Wisconsin. Adding to the significance of this view is the confluence of the Wisconsin River and the Mississippi. Look at the mud islands generated by the speedy waters of the Wisconsin River as it merges into the Mississippi.

$\mathcal{W}$inter in the Midwest hides outstanding and unusual surprises. Today, everything seems to be frozen, including my fingers on the shutter release.

Despite my trembling feet, shivers and the onset of frostbite, I am enjoying this same scene from Pikes Peak. The frozen Mississippi connects Iowa and

Wisconsin. Freezing is only one state of existence. Just beneath that ice flows the water of the river, continuing its trip south.

$\mathcal{W}$yalusing, Wisconsin: No wonder that Native Americans chose this place for their loved ones to rest in peace and eternity! What more peaceful, soothing, and inspiring view can anyone experience. Wyalusing State Park is a jubilee of mist, beauty, and reflective sights. No matter where we look — toward McGregor, Prairie du Chien, Marquette, the confluence of the Mississippi and Wisconsin rivers, or the backwaters and ravines — we see a gem. I share with you the same location with different looks — with winter's snow and ice trading places with the lush green.

*C*assville, Wisconsin: When you start driving to the top of the park, you get glimpses of the hilly terrain hiding behind the thick woods along the road. At its pinnacle you experience the captivating beauty of the river edged by the hills, ridges, ravines and lagoons prevalent in the area. It gets better. Walk down the cliffs and peer into the valley. You see an ideal example of the rural, simple life in Wisconsin. In addition to the Alliant Energy plant, I see few houses, barns and sheds hidden in the woods. Close enough to form a neighborhood, yet far enough to have privacy. Peaceful and inspiring. This view is visible only from this lower cliff in the park.

otosi, Wisconsin: On the Wisconsin side of the Mississippi, in the neighborhood of Potosi and Cassville, Rafic and I climb up a steep hill. For a minute we are trying to identify the towns whose bluffs appear in the background. Soon Rafic has the answer: "Dad, we are seeing your favorite hills of Iowa." Yes, it is Sherrill, Balltown, Buena Vista ("Buenie", as the locals call it). We are seeing them for the first time from this perspective. The Wisconsin bluffs gear down to touch the river, and the railroad tracks look like a neatly combed part in hair. Iowa's side of the river spreads the little towns that glitter on its bluffs. This scene is not easy to find; we are happy to make it visible to you.

uttenberg, Iowa: Driving the highway in Guttenberg will reveal a typical American city: car dealerships, fast-food restaurants, gas stations, industry, convenience stores, and the like. This is not all the story that Guttenberg can tell. The town has hidden attractions that you just have to discover. A few streets from the highway, you will see the river with a wealth of great restaurants, boutiques, art stores and other gems. From above, the city shows a fabulous panorama. This scene captures the upper view of Guttenberg with the Wisconsin bluffs also visible. In the second scene, the mist of fall surrounds the city with warmth and charm. Whatever the season, whatever the dress, Guttenberg displays its special beauty.

Galena, Illinois: On a crisp and invigorating fall morning in ascend into the heavens in a hot-air balloon we absorb the majesty of America's Heartland. The breeze floats us toward Galena. The wind then pauses, permitting us extra time to breathe in this view, which captures historic downtown Galena, the bluffs of Iowa, and the fog of the mighty Mississippi hugging the city.

Dubuque, Iowa: Looking west from the East Dubuque, Illinois, bluffs, your eyes cannot miss the sight of Dubuque, Iowa. The glittering lights from the river walk spread across the shores of the Mississippi and reflect back to Illinois. The Dubuque shoreline is vibrant, with parties and meetings in the Grand River Center serving as a focal point. Take a stroll along Dubuque's River Walk; you will be happy with the experience.

*D*ubuque, Iowa: Mount Carmel, the motherhouse of the Sisters of Charity of the Blessed Virgin Mary, possesses this spectacular northward view of the Mississippi River. I go there often to relax and enjoy this Gestalt view. Shortly after sunrise, I stand behind the tree to capture this scene. It was an amazing moment, as I could hide from the sun but yet witness its light wrapping around the trunk. From this vantage point, I can see the courthouse dome, the railroad tracks and rail cars on the siding, the bluffs of Dubuque, the Julien Dubuque Bridge, and the Mighty River bisecting the entire scene. The picture does not show all that I have seen; it is the next best thing to being there.

Dubuque, Iowa: It is not a metaphoric exaggeration. Always — yes always — my heart pounds when I see Dubuque from the Iowa-Wisconsin bridge. I love Dubuque. It is my home, my family, and my American Dream. Yes, this great nation has given me all the opportunities to be who I am now and to become who I want to be in the future. But my love for Dubuque does not cause me to overstate its beauty! This town has so much beauty, there is no need for cosmetics or embellishments. In this scene, we see the interplay of the Mississippi's main channel and backwaters. The oval islands, the bluffs, and the beautiful blue of the river write a legend of peace and tranquility. Come and visit Dubuque. Likewise, I call on Dubuquers to do the same!

Dubuque, Iowa

ubuque, Iowa: As I take this panorama, my dad is in La Crosse, Wisconsin. Though he is not with me in person, his spirit is ever-present. Dad's enthusiasm, creativity, and perspective inspire my imagination. On this day, my imagination is carried away. As I approach an overlook from Dubuque's historic Eagle Point Park, I see a southbound barge passing below the Iowa-Wisconsin Bridge. Dubuque's American Lady follows closely behind. I see the bluffs shine with a kiss of the sun's rays and the river sparkling with life. Simply breathtaking! I run to the car and grab my camera; I want to capture every single second of this inspiring experience.

Dubuque, Iowa

Dubuque, Iowa

Kieler, Wisconsin

$\mathcal{B}$alltown, Iowa: All the elements of arts are there — an art that no human hand can imitate. The gold of the corn, the green of the earth, the blue of the water, and the peaceful country life. It is like a dream. The Mississippi River, in the background, connects Iowa and Wisconsin. The overlook from Balltown, beckons visitors to this work of art.

$\mathcal{B}$ellevue, Iowa: No matter how often I visit Bellevue, I always see in it a new way. Its name translates to "beautiful view," and, to me, it is among the 10 most beautiful cities on the mighty Mississippi. The geography of the small city, the simple historic architecture, and the great community make it a gift from and to the river. If I let my emotions speak, I would fill these pages without sufficiently describing its beauty.

abula, Iowa: No, this is not computer-enhanced. This is
the real art that God has given Sabula, this tiny Iowa town
on the Mississippi. I see a classical painting, but it is not in
the museum but in real life. The clouds and the river merge
at the horizon to sign an unprecedented piece of eternal art.

Fulton, Illinois

avenport, Iowa: Elements of beauty are countless. Time, form, colors and light act in concert at the Centennial Bridge. The sky gripped the last of the sun's rays, which cascaded over the span, seemingly converting steel into gold. The shimmering lights weaved a golden garment for the Mississippi as it flows beneath the Centennial, linking Davenport with Rock Island, Illinois.

Davenport, Iowa

Davenport, Iowa

Burlington, Iowa: Lighted bridges are not bridges only. They are beautiful and romantic. They do not reflect only light and color. They reflect the character of the cities that host them. Throughout our travel along the Mississippi, we have observed that lighted bridges did not only invite us, but they just as much invite their local residents to enjoy their beautiful locations both day and night. To the left, a romancing couple takes in the beautiful colors of Burlington's bridge as reflected upon the Mississippi. We hope more cities will light their bridges.

Quincy, Illinois

*H*annibal, Missouri: Yes, Mark Twain, I see what you see every day. I see the barges, the boats, the factory, and the bridges. I hear the whispering winds bringing to you the latest stories of the river. I note the silence in your sculpture — those quiet moments you always wanted. Hannibal is great, but it is greater as it hosts your name in each and every venue. Restaurants, museums, theaters, parks, schools, apartment houses, hotels – all want your name. And Rafic and I want you in our book. Mark, so many people have passed by Hannibal and the Mississippi, however, none of them could give the river and the town what you did.

$\mathcal{L}$ ittle Dixie Highway, Missouri: Leaving Hannibal and heading to St. Louis, we take the Little Dixie Highway. The hilly and picturesque road invites us to capture its scenic views. Farther down the ridges, the trees on each of the river's banks form a fascinating colorful carpet. The river narrows, then again widens, adding movement and patterns.

$\mathcal{S}$t. Louis, Missouri: Through the lens, I witness a grand view of the Mississippi River and the famous Gateway Arch. I wanted to capture the symbiotic relationship of the arch and river, as they symbolize America's growth, culture, and history. From this angle, I see the arch standing in salute to a river serving the recreational, cultural and economic needs of this great nation.

Alton, Illinois

$\mathcal{C}$olumbus, Kentucky: Shortly after sunset we arrive here, at a beautiful park. The hint of red tint over the water formed a thin layer of mystic light that reaches directly to the heart. "Rafic! Rafic!" He was not within sight or sound! I worry, because in this place he should be able to hear me from miles away. I repeat my call. No answer! I finally find him at the other side of the park, in his own world while taking extended-exposure shots of the Mississippi about to merge with the Ohio River.

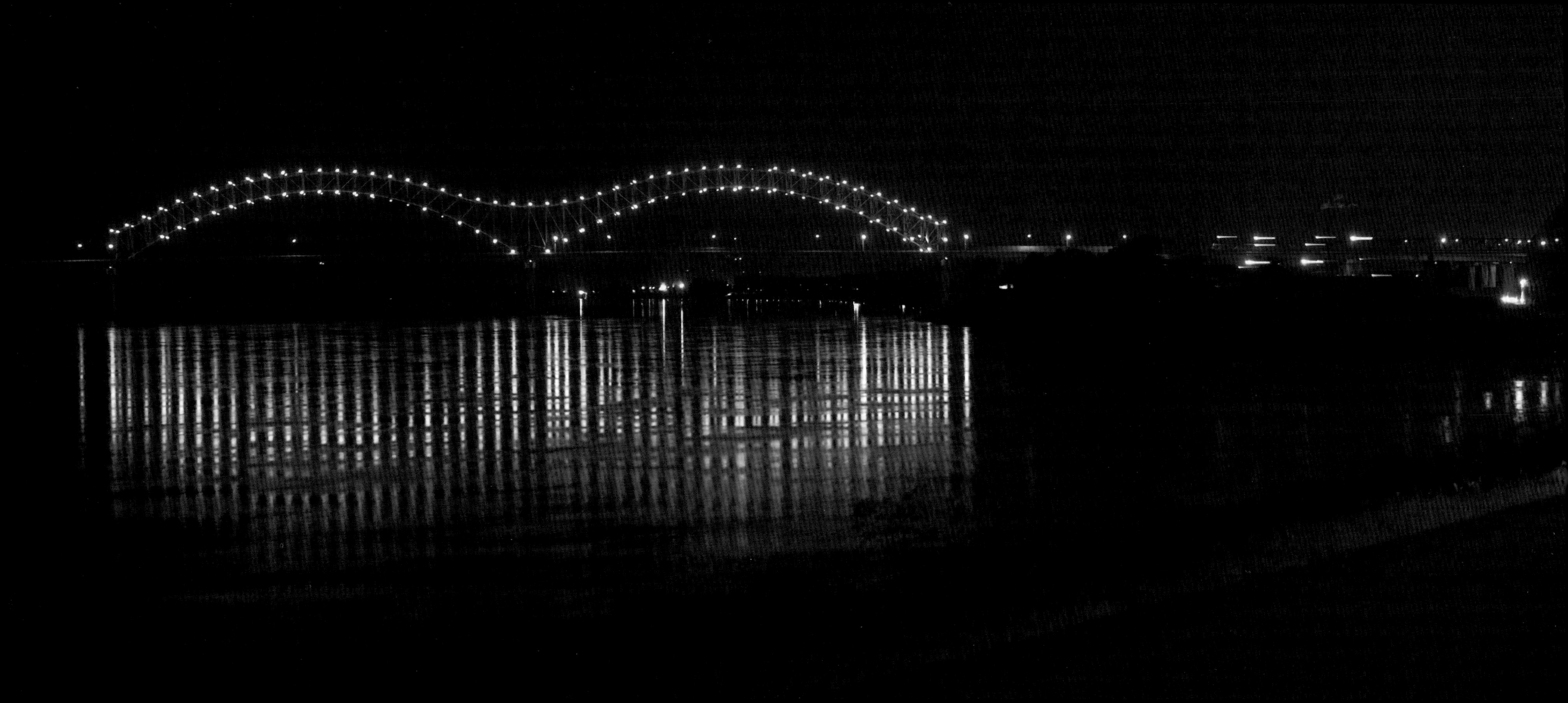

$\mathcal{M}$emphis, Tennessee: How often you search and don't find, and how often you don't search and find! Memphis' portion on the Mississippi is nothing short of breathtaking. During the day, one cannot miss its cityscapes, architecture, and culture, combined with its charm, power, and pride. Memphis nights have a different story to tell; it is the tale of the Mississippi with its gentle waves playing its symphony of grace on the organ of light.

Lake Village, Arkansas

Vicksburg, Mississippi: General U.S. Grant is right here, standing where I am. Rafic starts telling me what he learned about the Civil War and General Grant when he attended Hempstead High School in Dubuque, Iowa. Grant once lived just a dozen miles from Dubuque. Comparing notes, I remember what I learned about Grant and that war when I studied in Beirut, Lebanon. Yes, great nations and great people are the heritage of the entire world; not only their respective nations.

$\mathcal{N}$atchez, Mississippi: The parks on the bluffs are among the most beautiful we have seen. We capture this view from a hilly area that overlooks Vidalia, Louisiana, and Natchez, Mississippi. We note the interplay of the blue and muddy waters of the Mississippi River as two barges pass.

Baton Rouge, Louisiana

New Orleans, Louisiana

New Orleans, Louisiana: Yes, New Orleans, I am ecstatic in your presence. I am amazed, overwhelmed and in love. It is 4 a.m., and I am feeling her unprecedented beauty consuming my heart and soul. Many thought that Hurricane Katrina had brought your end. They were wrong. You have proven to the universe that beauty wins over ugliness. That perseverance wins over surrender. And that sweetness wins over bitterness.

Pilottown, Louisiana: Katrina was here! We see the aftermath. Katrina damaged structures, trees, walls, roofs, and landscapes. Pilottown was Katrina's playground. However, Pilottown proved stronger than Katrina. The storm is gone, but Pilottown remains. The boats are back, the fishermen stop by the restaurant for a treat, the blue Mississippi eternally hugs the island with love and beauty. Fascinated with the beauty, perseverance, and heritage of Pilottown, we document a legendary island that refused to surrender. We leave Pilottown with beautiful memories engraved in our minds and hearts.

The Mississippi Southwest Pass, Louisiana: Gulf of Mexico, our last destination is where the Mississippi merges with the Gulf of Mexico. It is late afternoon when we start our trip toward the gulf. Rafic and I are hoping to get there before sunset, but it is questionable whether we will make it in time. I ask Chad, our charter boat owner, "How powerful are your engines?" "Two-hundred-fifty horsepower I have," he says. "Do you have spurs for all of them?" He looks forward without an answer. The back of the boat, where Rafic and I sit, approaches the surface, forming two white wings of beading water that splash like pearls as they hit the sun. The nose of the boat rises to around 45 degrees, and our gear slides all the way back, next to our feet. On our way we were to our final destination. I see Rafic's face glowing with gold, white, and mist. The wind is strong, but neither of us even wants to blink. We do not want to miss a moment. Chad knows exactly where to take us. He points to the old, abandoned lighthouse on a narrow stretch of land. The ocean appears, and Chad tells us that we were lucky that it's not muddy. Yes, it is a magical mix of darker and lighter blues, mixed with a mysterious and mesmerizing yellow. The sun is setting, leaving a white reflection on the mix. We don't have enough of this mystic scene formed by the unity of the ocean, Mississippi River, and us.

Index

Lake Itasca, MN 6-7
Bemidji, MN 8-9
Grand Rapids, MN 10-11
Brainerd, MN 12-13
Sauk Rapids, MN 14-15
St. Cloud, MN 16-17
Minneapolis, MN 18-21
St. Paul, MN 22-23
Red Wing, MN 24-25
Lake City, MN 26
Pepin, WI 27
Alma, WI 28-29
Dakota, MN 30-31
Winona, MN 32-33
Trempealeau, WI 34-35
Onalaska, MN 36-39
La Crosse, WI 40-43
Lansing, IA 44-45
McGregor, IA 46-47
Wyalusing, WI 48-49
Cassville, WI 50-51
Potosi, WI 52-53
Guttenberg, IA 54-55

Galena, IL 56-57
Dubuque, IA 58-71
Kieler, WI 72-73
Balltown, IA 74-75
Bellevue, IA 76-77
Sabula, IA 78-79
Fulton, IL 80-81
Davenport, IA 82-87
Burlington, IA 88-89
Quincy, IL 90-91
Hannibal, MO 92-93
Little Dixie Highway, MO 94-95
St. Louis, MO 96-97
Alton, IL 98-99
Columbus, KY 100-101
Memphis, TN 102-103
Lake Village, AR 104-105
Vicksburg, MS 106-107
Natchez, MS 108-109
Baton Rouge, LA 110-111
New Orleans, LA 112-115
Pilottown, LA 116-117
Southwest Pass, LA 118-119

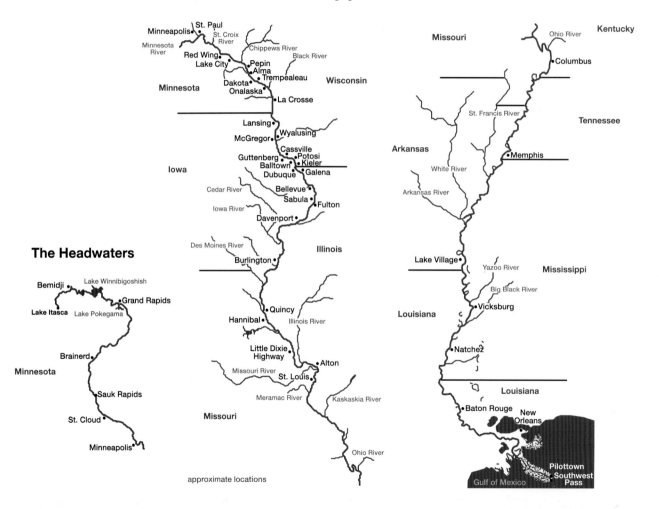

The Mississippi River

The Headwaters

approximate locations